£2.95

Wolfgang Amadeus Mozart

CONCERTI FOR WIND INSTRUMENTS

in Full Score

Dover Publications, Inc., New York

Published in Canada by General Publishing Company, Ltd.,
30 Lesmill Road, Don Mills, Toronto, Ontario.
Published in the United Kingdom by Constable and Company,
Ltd.

This Dover edition, first published in 1986, is an unabridged
republication of *Serie 12. Zweite Abtheilung. Concerte für ein Blasinstrument
und Orchester* (Series 12. Second Section. Concerti for One Wind Instrument
and Orchestra), 1881, from *Wolfgang Amadeus Mozart's Werke. Kritisch durch-
gesehene Gesammtausgabe*, Breitkopf & Härtel, Leipzig, 1877–1883.

Manufactured in the United States of America
Dover Publications, Inc., 31 East 2nd Street
Mineola, N.Y. 11501

Library of Congress Cataloging-in-Publication Data
Mozart, Wolfgang Amadeus, 1756–1791.
[Instrumental music. Selections]
Concerti for wind instruments.

Originally published: Leipzig : Breitkopf & Härtel,
1877–1883.
Contents: For bassoon in B-flat major, K. 191—
For flute and harp in C major, K. 299—For flute in G
major, K. 313—[etc.]
1. Concertos—Scores.   2. Flute with orchestra—
Scores.   I. Mozart, Wolfgang Amadeus, 1756–1791.
Concertos. Selections. 1986.   II. Mozart, Wolfgang
Amadeus, 1756–1791. Andantes, flute, orchestra,
K. 315, C major. 1986.
M1004.5.M7I62   1986   86-753154
ISBN 0-486-25228-0

CONTENTS

Concerto for Bassoon in B-flat Major, K.191

1

6   *Concerto for Bassoon, K.191*

14 *Concerto for Bassoon, K.191*

Concerto for Flute and Harp in C Major, K.299

Rondo.

Concerto for Flute in G Major, K.313

Concerto for Flute in D Major, K.314

122   *Concerto for Flute, K.314*

Andante for Flute and Orchestra
in C Major, K.315

Concerto for Horn in D Major, K.412

SOLO

Concerto for Horn in E-flat Major, K.417

SOLO.

154 *Concerto for Horn, K.417*

RONDO.
SOLO

TUTTI

Più Allegro.

166　*Concerto for Horn, K.417*

Concerto for Horn in E-flat Major, K.447

Romanze.

Larghetto.

Concerto for Horn in E-flat Major, K.495

ROMANZA.
Andante.

RONDO.
Allegro vivace.

Concerto for Horn, K.495

Concerto for Clarinet in A Major, K.622

212 *Concerto for Clarinet, K.622*

214   *Concerto for Clarinet, K.622*